KONTEMPORARY AMERIKAN POETRY:POEMS

Also by John Murillo

Up Jump the Boogie

KONTEMPORARY AMERIKAN POETRY:POEMS

John Murillo

Four Way Books
Tribeca

for Nicole

and in loving memory
of Josefina Cervantes Murillo,
Francisco Morales Santiago,
and Philip Levine

Library of Congress Cataloging-in-Publication Data

Names: Murillo, John, author.
Title: Kontemporary Amerikan poetry / John Murillo.
Description: New York : Four Way Books, [2020]
Identifiers: LCCN 2019031752 | ISBN 9781945588471 (trade paperback)
Classification: LCC PS3613.U6945 A6 2020 | DDC 811/.6--dc23
LC record available at https://lccn.loc.gov/2019031752

This book is manufactured in the United States of America and printed on
acid-free paper.
3rd printing, 2020
Four Way Books is a not-for-profit literary press. We are grateful for the assistance
we receive from individual donors, public arts agencies, and private foundations.

This publication is made possible with public funds from the
National Endowment for the Arts

and from the New York State Council on the Arts, a state agency,

We are a proud member of the Community of Literary Magazines and Presses.

[clmp]

CONTENTS

"I know this isn't much.
But I wanted to explain this life to you, even if
I had to become, over the years, someone else to do it."
—Larry Levis

"'You're lying,' said Memory.
'You're asleep,' said Forgetfulness."
—Henry Dumas

ON CONFESSIONALISM

Not sleepwalking, but waking still,
   with my hand on a gun, and the gun
in a mouth, and the mouth
   on the face of a man on his knees.
Autumn of '89, and I'm standing
   in a Section 8 apartment parking lot,
pistol cocked, and staring down
   at this man, then up into the mug
of an old woman staring, watering
   the single sad flower to the left
of her stoop, the flower also staring.
   My engine idling behind me, a slow
moaning bassline and the bark
   of a dead rapper nudging me on.
All to say, someone's brokenhearted.
   And this man with the gun in his mouth—
this man who, like me, is really little
   more than a boy—may or may not
have something to do with it.
   May or may not have said a thing
or two, betrayed a secret, say,
   that walked my love away. And why
not say it: She adored me. And I,
   her. More than anyone, anything

in life, up to then, and then still,

   for two decades after. And, therefore,

went for broke. Blacked out and woke

   having gutted my piggy and pawned

all my gold to buy what a homeboy

   said was a Beretta. Blacked out

and woke, my hand on a gun, the gun

   in a mouth, a man, who was really

a boy, on his knees. And because

   I loved the girl, I actually paused

before I pulled the trigger—once,

   twice, three times—then panicked

not just because the gun jammed,

   but because what if it hadn't,

because who did I almost become,

   there, that afternoon, in a Section 8

apartment parking lot, pistol cocked,

   with the sad flower staring, because

I knew the girl I loved—no matter

   how this all played out—would never

have me back. Day of damaged ammo,

   or grime that clogged the chamber.

Day of faulty rods, or springs come

   loose in my fist. Day nobody died,

so why not *Hallelujah*? Say *Amen* or
   Thank you? My mother sang for years
of God, babes, and fools. My father,
   lymph node masses fading from
his x-rays, said surviving one thing
   means another comes and kills you.
He's dead, and so, I trust him. Dead,
   and so I'd wonder, years, about the work
I left undone—boy on his knees
   a man now, risen, and likely plotting
his long way back to me. Fuck it.
   I tucked my tool like the movie gangsters
do, and jumped back in my bucket.
   Cold enough day to make a young man
weep, afternoon when everything,
   or nothing, changed forever. The dead
rapper grunted, the bassline faded,
   my spirits whispered something
from the trees. I left, then lost the pistol
   in a storm drain, somewhere between
that life and this. Left the pistol in
   a storm drain, but never got around
to wiping away the prints.

I

VARIATION ON A THEME BY ELIZABETH BISHOP

Start with loss. Lose everything. Then lose it all again.
Lose a good woman on a bad day. Find a better woman,
then lose five friends chasing her. Learn to lose as if
your life depended on it. Learn that your life depends on it.
Learn it like karate, like riding a bike. *Learn it, master it.*
Lose money, lose time, lose your natural mind.
Get left behind, then learn to leave others. Lose and
lose again. Measure a father's coffin against a cousin's
crashing T-cells. Kiss your sister through prison glass.
Know why your woman's not answering her phone.
Lose sleep. Lose religion. Lose your wallet in El Segundo.
Open your window. Listen: the last slow notes
of a Donny Hathaway song. A child crying. Listen:
a drunk man is cussing out the moon. He sounds like
your dead uncle, who, before he left, lost a leg
to sugar. Shame. Learn what's given can be taken;
what can be taken, will. This you can bet on without
losing. Sure as nightfall and an empty bed. Lose
and lose again. Lose until it's second nature. *Losing
farther, losing faster.* Lean out your open window, listen:
the child is laughing now. No, it's the drunk man again
in the street, losing his voice, suffering each invisible star.

UPON READING THAT ERIC DOLPHY TRANSCRIBED EVEN THE CALLS OF CERTAIN SPECIES OF BIRDS,

I think first of two sparrows I met when walking home,
late night years ago, in another city, not unlike this—the one

bird frantic, attacking I thought, the way she swooped
down, circled my head, and flailed her wings in my face;

how she seemed to scream each time I swung; how she
dashed back and forth between me and a blood-red Corolla

parked near the opposite curb; how, finally, I understood:
I spied another bird, also calling, his foot inexplicably

caught in the car's closed door, beating his whole bird
body against it. Trying, it appeared, to bang himself free.

And who knows how long he'd been there, flailing. Who
knows—he and the other I mistook, at first, for a bat.

They called to me—something between squawk and chirp,
something between song and prayer—to do something,

anything. And, like any good god, I disappeared. Not
indifferent, exactly. But with things to do. And, most likely,

on my way home from another heartbreak. Call it 1997,
and say I'm several thousand miles from home. By which

I mean those were the days I made of everyone a love song.
By which I mean I was lonely and unrequited. But that's

not quite it either. Truth is, I did manage to find a few
to love me, but couldn't always love them back. The Rasta

law professor. The firefighter's wife. The burlesque dancer
whose daughter blackened drawings with *m*'s to mean

the sky was full of birds the day her daddy died. I think
his widow said he drowned one morning on a fishing trip.

Anyway, I'm digressing. But if you asked that night—
did I mention it was night?—why I didn't even try

to jimmy the lock to spring the sparrow, I couldn't say,
truthfully, that it had anything to do with envy, with wanting

a woman to plead as deeply for me as these sparrows did,
one for the other. No. I'd have said something, instead,

about the neighborhood itself, the car thief shot a block
and a half east the week before. Or about the men

I came across nights prior, sweat-slicked and shirtless,
grappling in the middle of the street, the larger one's chest

pressed to the back of the smaller, bruised and bleeding
both. I know you thought this was about birds,

but stay with me. I left them both in the street—
the same street where I'd leave the sparrows—the men

embracing and, for all one knows (especially one not
from around there), they could have been lovers—

the one whispering an old, old, tune into the ear
of the other—*Baby, baby, don't leave me this way.* I left

the men where I'd leave the sparrows and their song.
And as I walked away, I heard one of the men call to me,

please or *help* or *brother* or some such. And I didn't break
stride, not one bit. It's how I've learned to save myself.

Let me try this another way. Call it 1977. And say
I'm back west, south central Los Angeles. My mother

and father at it again. But this time in the street,
broad daylight, and all the neighbors watching. One,

I think his name was Sonny, runs out from his duplex
to pull my father off. You see where I'm going with this.

My mother crying out, fragile as a sparrow. Sonny
fighting my father, fragile as a sparrow. And me,

years later, trying to get it all down. As much for you—
I'm saying—as for me. Sonny catches a left, lies flat

on his back, blood starting to pool and his own
wife wailing. My mother wailing, and traffic backed,

now, half a block. Horns, whistles, and soon sirens.
1977. Summer. And all the trees full of birds. Hundreds,

I swear. And since I'm the one writing it, I'll tell you
they were crying. Which brings me back to Dolphy

and his transcribing. The jazzman, I think, wanted only
to get it down pure. To get it down exact—the animal

wracking itself against a car's steel door, the animals
in the trees reporting, the animals we make of ourselves

and one another. Flailing, failing. Stay with me now.
Days after the dustup, my parents took me to the park.

And in this park was a pond, and in this pond were birds.
Not sparrows, but swans. And my father spread a blanket

and brought from a basket some apples and a paring knife.
Summertime. My mother wore sunglasses. And long sleeves.

My father, now sober, cursed himself for leaving the radio.
But my mother forgave him, and said, as she caressed

the back of his hand, that we could just listen to the swans.
And we listened. And I watched. Two birds coupling,

one beating its wings as it mounted the other. Summer,
1977. I listened. And watched. When my parents made love

late into that night, I covered my ears in the next room,
scanning the encyclopedia for swans. It meant nothing to me—

then, at least—but did you know the collective noun
for swans is a *lamentation*? And is a lamentation not

its own species of song? What a woman wails, punch drunk
in the street? Or what a widow might sing, learning her man

was drowned by swans? A lamentation of them? Imagine
the capsized boat, the panicked man, struck about the eyes,

nose, and mouth each time he comes up for air. Imagine
the birds coasting away and the waters suddenly calm.

Either trumpet swans or mutes. The dead man's wife
running for help, crying to any who'd listen. A lamentation.

And a city busy saving itself. I'm digressing, sure. But
did you know that to digress means to stray from the flock?

When I left my parents' house, I never looked back. By which
I mean I made like a god and disappeared. As when I left

the sparrows. And the copulating swans. As when someday
I'll leave this city. Its every flailing, its every animal song.

ON METAPHOR

In back of daddy's closet,
behind the cold and loaded
pistol, I find a cedar box
of snapshots—his company
in camouflage, waving rifles,
reefer, and middle fingers
at the photographer. At you.
And at me. And here,
the full-lipped redbone
he left in the world without
a goodbye. Here, a strange
boy with my father's forehead,
same sullen eyes. Flip the photo:
a stranger's name and dates
that don't add, scrawled as if
rushed, as if a fugitive's note
slipped quick to the future.
When my mother walks in,
I shove the box to the back
of the shelf, say nothing
of the redbone or the boy.
I hand her, instead, the pistol.
A .45, I believe. Its cold barrel
swelling in the room's bum

light. When she angles it,
just so, I think I see my father
reflected in the steel. Wait, no—
Not my father. It's me.

DOLORES, MAYBE.

I've never spoken to anyone about this. Until now, until you.

I slept once in a field beyond the riverbank,
a flock of nightjars watching over me.

That was the summer a farmer found his daughter
hanging in the hayloft, and wished, for the first time,
he had not touched her so.

I wish I could say we were close—the girl and I,
I mean—but only knew her to wave hello,

and walked her, once, halfway up the road
before turning finally into my grandmother's yard.

This was Ontario, California. 1983.
Which is to say, there was no river.
And I wouldn't know a nightjar if it bit me.

But the girl was real. And the day they found her, that was real.

And the dress she wore, same as on our walk—
periwinkle, she called it; I called it blue,
blue with bright yellow flowers all over

—the dress and the flowers, they too were real.

And on our walk, I remember, we cut through the rail yard,
and came upon a dead coyote lying near the tracks.

A frail and dusty heap of regret, he was companion to no one.

Stone still, staring. Our shadows stretched long and covering the animal.
She told me something, I want to say, about loneliness.

Something I've since forgotten, the way I've forgotten—
though I can see her face as if she were standing right here—her very name.

Let's call her *Dolores*, from *dolor*. Spanish for *anguish*.

And whatever the sky, however lovely that afternoon,
I remember mostly the wind,
how a breeze unraveled what was left of a braid,

and when I tried to brush from Dolores's brow
a few loose strands, how she flinched,
how she ran the rest of the way home,

how I never saw her after that,
except when they carried her from the barn—her periwinkle dress,
her blue legs and arms, and the fields
ablaze with daisies.

I spent the rest of that summer in the rail yard
with my dead coyote, watching trains loaded and leaving.

All summer long, I'd pelt him with stones.
All summer long, I'd use the stones to spell the girl's name—
Dolores, maybe—in the dirt.

All summer long, fire ants crawled over and between each letter—
her name, now, its own small town.

A season of heat and heavy rains washed my coyote to nothing.
Only teeth and a few stubborn bones

that refused, finally, to go down.

Weeks into autumn, someone found the father
hanged from the same groaning tie-beams,
the hayloft black with bottle flies.

But that was 1983. Ontario, California.

Which is to say, the bottle flies are dead. So, too, the ants.

And neither field nor barn is where I left it.

I've never spoken to anyone about this. Until now, until you.

I gathered a handful of my coyote's bones, his teeth,

and strung them all on fishing wire—

a talisman to ward off anguish. A talisman I hold out to you now.

Please. Come closer. Take this from my hand.

ON MAGICAL REALISM
—Ontario, CA. 1981

Stained with rosaries
     and skeletons, some
virgin or another praying
     on his shoulder, Tiny
shuffles toward and
     leans heavy, as if trying,
into the first perfect hook
     my father will land that summer,
and miles north, Tiny's mother
     clutches her chest, hearing
just then, on a dusty mantle
     in an empty room, framed
glass crack and crack again
     just along the left jawline
of a favorite baby boy
     who will grow into a man
who calls a man *Nigger,*
     in a room full of niggers,
and the nigger with the hook—
     my father—asks *What's my name,*
What's my name, What's
     my motherfucking name?

as the photo frame

      shatters damn near to dust,

Tiny's mother buckles

      and she cries, *God...*

POEM ENDING AND BEGINNING ON LINES BY LARRY LEVIS

Because you haven't praised anything in months,
and because iron, because two ten-pound plates—
when pressed to six wheels and late sets—are enough
to drive better men to dust, and because the young bucks
curling near the mirror have paused their pretty work
to watch your old ass snatch from the bench's
buckling uprights all three hundred and thirty-five
goddam pounds, you summon the saint of iron,
the blacksmith in palm skirt fisting his machetes,
to give you just a little bit of what you need to bring it
down, to bang it up, just once. Just this once.
—*Ago, Baba Mi. Ogun Owanile O, Ogun, Cobu Cobu.*

Of course, the young bucks chuckle at this ooga-booga
babble, this strange ritual gibberish of an old-timer,
obviously—in the parlance of the place—dead set
to fuck his self up. But you break the weight, you do.
And the room falls quiet save the quiver and clang
of iron on iron, the few slim seconds it takes to turn
back time. Lift off, and you're a young man in an old city.
No beard, no gray. Lift again, and Parliament is pulsing
from a ghetto blaster perched on a pair of milk crates
in a neighbor's yellow yard, your sixteen-year-old self
is writhing under another bar, what feels like two tons

crushing you dead, and Robert Caldwell's glaring
from behind the bench, yelling for you to drive it all up.

Robert Caldwell, barrel-chested, chiseled, and damn
near three hundred pounds, who pushed a pallet jack
for twelve-hour shifts, after twenty-something years
stretched across San Quentin, Soledad, and Folsom;
Robert Caldwell, the triple O.G., who once threatened
his boss with a box-cutter for wolfing loud, or holding
eye contact a little too long, has for reasons unknown
chosen you for his pet project, promising to forge you
into something unbreakable. Said by summer's end,
you, too, will have grown men flinching when you flex,
and the women—*oh, the women*—will make disappear
all the deep deep ache a man inflicts on himself. Or,
rather, all the pain Robert Caldwell will inflict on you.
For make no mistake, this will be a summer that hurts.

Deadlifts, box squats, power cleans, and curls.
The egg yolks' nasty, the slither down your throat.
Drop sets, pyramids, twenty-ones, and cheats. The day
you learned how Robert Caldwell found his father
dead. Days dead the day before, a stolen Desert Eagle
spent and sprawled near what once was a face.

Robert Caldwell drops this on you hard between sets,
but doesn't pause to break down sobbing. *Push, nigga.
Push,* says Robert Caldwell. *Pain is weakness leaving.*
Push, nigga. Push. Become something unbreakable.
Robert Caldwell doesn't break or take a day to mourn,
or ring your phone late night to chat about regret,
or counsel you to love better than you've been.
He does what any good ironworker does. He works.

And he works you. All summer long. Sets and reps
and pressure and flame and all the requisite ache.
You don't break, exactly, but come close to buckling.
That summer, and summers since. So much burn,
so much weight. So much. You'll leave three women,
the rest will leave you first. You'll bury your own father,
lose four friends to gunfire, one to a jailhouse noose.
Your hands will shame you often. But first, this.
O.G. Robert Caldwell, his jigs, blocks, and hammer.
O.G. Robert Caldwell, backlit by the sun. *Ogun
Owanile O, Ogun Cobu Cobu.* How beautiful this man,
his trust in iron, what it gives us, what it takes.
What it gives again. He yells for you to push, you push.

Robert Caldwell, you think, would have loved this
beat down Brooklyn hole in the wall, its ripped leather
seatbacks, all its stale air. He'd have loved the rusty
dumbbells, the dirt-caked mirror, the young bucks
circling you now, watching and waiting. You stare hard
into that mirror, into your beard and gray. Crow's feet
and furrows. Thirty-something summers and you've become
the triple O.G. Every ache you've earned tells you so.
The young bucks clock you as you lay back on the bench,
your hands chalked and finding their grip. *Weight,*
you think, *they don't have a clue.* You break the bar
from its rack, feel it all bearing down. The quiver and heft,
the sudden, overcast quiet of the past tense.

DEAR YUSEF,

Again last night, I caught Medusa
    sitting in my living room.
Not the devil. Not the dog
    in the shadows, made of shadows.
Not the old translucent maroon
    sharpening his machete. But
Medusa, lighting a spliff, spreading
    tarot cards across the floor.
I didn't startle when a door slammed
    but half expected a black cat
to run over my shoes. She wore
    the same red lipstick as the night
before, Yusef. Same black teddy
    with the skinny strap slipped
from her shoulder. Singing to herself,
    her voice split in two—contralto,
baritone: balladeer stroking the braids
    of a woman everyone knows
he beats; the woman singing *Yes*
    and *It's alright...* Sequined sleeves
hiding every track, a disco ball
    scattering shards of light along
some drab and peeling wall—Medusa
    cut the deck, relit the spliff, flipped

29

one card, then another. Took a pull
   so long I thought she'd catch fire.
You've not always been a good man,
   she said, showing seven cards,
coughing hard. There was something
   she wasn't telling me. She liked
that I didn't ask. Liked how I watched
   her dusting ashes from her thigh.
I see trouble finds you easy, hey boy?
   I pulled her onto my lap, or I slid
myself, somehow, up under her
   —I can't remember which—
she singing *Yes,* and *It's alright…*
   then slipping the joint, fire side first,
between her lips, she took my face
   in her hands, and shotgunned a cloud
into my open mouth. Some nights,
   Yusef, the serpents curse my name.
Some nights, they tell me secrets.

ON NEGATIVE CAPABILITY

Whitewalls Mudflaps
Late night howling down
   a dark dirt road Headlights
killed and so the world gone
   black but for the two blunts
lit illuminating Jojo's fake gold
   grin One girl each screaming
from the backseat we raced
   the red moon rawdogged
the stars His mama's car
   my daddy's gun *Public Enemy*
Number One Seventeen and
   simple we wannabe hard-
rocks threw rudeboy fingers
   and gang signs at the sky
Blinded by the hot smoke
   rising like the sirens
in the subwoofers blinded
   by the crotchfunk rising
from all our eager selves We
   mashed in perfect murk a city
block's length at least
   toward God toward God
knows what when or why

neither Jojo nor I nor our
two dates screaming   had a clue
  or even care   what the black
ahead held
              Come road
  come night   come blackness
and the cold   Come havoc
  come mayhem   Come down
God   and see us   Come
  bloodshot moon running
alongside the ride as if
  to warn us away from as if
to run us straight into   some
  jagged tooth and jackal-throated
roadside ditch
              When Jojo
  gunned the gas we pushed into
that night like a nest of sleeping
  jaybirds shaken loose and
plunging   Between our screams
  a hush so heavy   we could
almost hear what was waiting
  in the dark

Publication of this book was made possible by grants and donations. We are also grateful to those individuals who participated in our 2019 Build a Book Program. They are:

Anonymous (14), Sally Ball, Vincent Bell, Jan Bender-Zanoni, Laurel Blossom, Adam Bohannon, Lee Briccetti, Jane Martha Brox, Anthony Cappo, Carla & Steven Carlson, Andrea Cohen, Janet S. Crossen, Marjorie Deninger, Patrick Donnelly, Charles Douthat, Morgan Driscoll, Lynn Emanuel, Blas Falconer, Monica Ferrell, Joan Fishbein, Jennifer Franklin, Sarah Freligh, Helen Fremont & Donna Thagard, Ryan George, Panio Gianopoulos, Lauri Grossman, Julia Guez, Naomi Guttman & Jonathan Mead, Steven Haas, Bill & Cam Hardy, Lori Hauser, Bill Holgate, Deming Holleran, Piotr Holysz, Nathaniel Hutner, Elizabeth Jackson, Rebecca Kaiser Gibson, Dorothy Tapper Goldman, Voki Kalfayan, David Lee, Howard Levy, Owen Lewis, Jennifer Litt, Sara London & Dean Albarelli, David Long, Ralph & Mary Ann Lowen, Jacquelyn Malone, Fred Marchant, Donna Masini, Louise Mathias, Catherine McArthur, Nathan McClain, Richard McCormick, Kamilah Aisha Moon, James Moore, Beth Morris, John Murillo & Nicole Sealey, Kimberly Nunes, Rebecca Okrent, Jill Pearlman, Marcia & Chris Pelletiere, Maya Pindyck, Megan Pinto, Barbara Preminger, Kevin Prufer, Martha Rhodes, Paula Rhodes, Silvia Rosales, Linda Safyan, Peter & Jill Schireson, Jason Schneiderman, Roni & Richard Schotter, Jane Scovell, Andrew Seligsohn & Martina Anderson, Soraya Shalforoosh, Julie A. Sheehan, James Snyder & Krista Fragos, Alice St. Claire-Long, Megan Staffel, Marjorie & Lew Tesser, Boris Thomas, Pauline Uchmanowicz, Connie Voisine, Martha Webster & Robert Fuentes, Calvin Wei, Bill Wenthe, Allison Benis White, Michelle Whittaker, Rachel Wolff, and Anton Yakovlev.

John Murillo is also the author of the poetry collection, *Up Jump the Boogie,* finalist for both the Kate Tufts Discovery Award and the PEN Open Book Award. His honors include a Pushcart Prize, two Larry Neal writers awards, the J. Howard and Barbara M. J. Wood Prize from the Poetry Foundation, and fellowships from the National Endowment for the Arts, the Bread Loaf Writers' Conference, Fine Arts Work Center in Provincetown, Cave Canem Foundation, the MacDowell Colony, and the Wisconsin Institute for Creative Writing. His poems have appeared in various journals and anthologies including *American Poetry Review, Poetry*, and *Best American Poetry 2017* and *2019*. He is an assistant professor of English at Wesleyan University and also teaches in the low-residency MFA program at Sierra Nevada College.

MERCY, MERCY ME

Crips, Bloods, and butterflies.
   A sunflower somehow planted
in the alley. Its broken neck.
   Maybe memory is all the home
you get. And rage, where you
   first learn how fragile the axis
upon which everything tilts.
   But to say you've come to terms
with a city that's never loved you
   might be overstating things a bit.
All you know is there was once
   a walk-up where now sits a lot,
vacant, and rats in deep grass
   hide themselves from the day.
That one apartment fire
   set back in '76—one the streets
called arson to collect a claim—
   could not do, ultimately, what
the city itself did, left to its own dank
   devices, some sixteen years later.
Rebellions, said some. Riots,
   said the rest. In any case, flames;
and the home you knew, ash.
   It's not an actual memory, but

you remember it still: a rust-
 bottomed Datsun handed down,
then stolen. Stripped, recovered,
 and built back from bolts.
Driving away in May. 1992.
 What's left of that life quivers
in the rearview—the world on fire,
 and half your head with it.

II

A REFUSAL TO MOURN THE DEATHS, BY GUNFIRE, OF THREE MEN IN BROOKLYN

"And at times, didn't the whole country try to break his skin?"
—*Tim Seibles*

You strike your one good match to watch its bloom
and jook, a swan song just before a night
wind comes to snuff it. That's the kind of day
it's been. Your Black & Mild, now, useless as
a prayer pressed between your lips. God damn
the wind. And everything it brings. You hit
the corner store to cop a light, and spy
the trouble rising in the cashier's eyes.
TV reports some whack job shot two cops
then popped himself, here, in the borough, just
one mile away. You've heard this one before.
In which there's blood. In which a black man snaps.
In which things burn. You buy your matches. Christ
is watching from the wall art, swathed in fire.

"This country is mine as much as an orphan's house is his."
—Terrance Hayes

To breathe it in, this boulevard perfume
of beauty shops and roti shacks, to take
in all its funk, calypso, reggaeton,
and soul, to watch school kids and elders go
about their days, their living, is, if not
to fall in love, at least to wonder why
some want us dead. Again this week, they killed
another child who looked like me. A child
we'll march about, who'll grace our placards, say,
then be forgotten like a trampled pamphlet. What
I want, I'm not supposed to. Payback. Woe
and plenty trouble for the gunman's clan.
I'm not supposed to. But I want a brick,
a window. One good match, to watch it bloom.

"America, I forgive you... I forgive you eating black children, I know your hunger."

—Bob Kaufman

You dream of stockpiles—bottles filled with gas
and wicks stripped from a dead cop's slacks—a row
of paddy wagons parked, a pitcher's arm.
You dream of roses, time-lapse blossoms from
the breasts of sheriffs, singing Calico,
and casings' rain. You dream of scattered stars,
dream panthers at the precinct, dream a black-
out, planned and put to use. You dream your crew
a getaway van, engine running. Or,
no thought to run at all. You dream a flare
sent up too late against the sky, the coup
come hard and fast. You dream of pistol smoke
and bacon, folded flags—and why feel shame?
Is it the dream? Or that it's only dream?

"& still when I sing this awful tale, there is more than a dead black man at the center."

—Reginald Dwayne Betts

You change the channel, and it's him again.
Or not him. Him, but younger. Him, but old.
Or him with skullcap. Kufi. Hoodied down.
It's him at fifteen. Him at forty. Bald,
or dreadlocked. Fat, or chiseled. Six foot three,
or three foot six. Coal black or Ralph Bunche bright.
Again, it's him. Again, he reached. Today,
behind his back, his waist, beneath the seat,
his socks, to pull an Uzi, morning star,
or Molotov. They said don't move, they said
get down, they said to walk back toward their car.
He, so to speak, got down… Three to the head,
six to the heart. A mother kneels and prays—
Not peace, but pipe bombs, hands to light the fuse.

"Fuck the whole muthafucking thing."
                                    —Etheridge Knight

A black man, dancing for the nightly news,
grins wide and white, all thirty-two aglow
and glad to be invited. Makes a show
of laying out, of laundry airing. Throws
the burden back on boys, their baggy wear
and boisterous voices. Tells good folk at home
how streets run bloody, riffraff take to crime
like mice to mayhem, and how lawmen, more
than ever, need us all to back them. Fuck
this chump, the channel, and the check they cut
to get him. Fuck the nodding blonde, the fat
man hosting. Fuck the story. Fuck the quick
acquittals. Fuck the crowds and camera van.
You change the channel. Fuck, it's him again.

"I enter this story by the same door each time."
—Julian Randall

At Normandy and Florence, brick in hand,
one afternoon in '92, with half
the city razed and turned against itself,
a young boy beat a man to meat and signed,
thereby, the Ledger of the Damned. Big Book
of Bad Decisions. Black Boy's Almanac
of Shit You Can't Take Back. We watched, in shock.
The fury, sure. But more so that it took
this long to set it. All these matchstick years…
He beat him with a brick, then danced a jig
around his almost-carcass. Cameras caught
him live and ran that loop for weeks, all night,
all day, to prove us all, I think, one thug,
one black beast prancing on the nightly news.

*"And when it comes to those hard deeds done by righteous people and martyrs,
isn't it about time for that to be you?"*
                                    —Gary Copeland Lilley

Not Huey on his high back wicker throne,
beret cocked cooler than an Oaktown pimp.
Or young Guevara marching into camp,
all swagger, mane, and slung M-1. But one
less suited, you could say, for picture books
and posters, slouching on a northbound Bolt,
caressing steel and posting plans to shoot.
He means, for once, to be of use. Small axe
to massive branches, tree where hangs the noose.
He says he's "putting wings on pigs today,"
wants two for each of us they've blown away.
Wants gun salutes and caskets. Dirges, tears,
and wreaths. Wants widows on the witness stand,
or near the riot's flashpoint, brick in hand.

"I itch for my turn."

         —Indigo Moor

Like Malcolm at the window, rifle raised
and ready for whatever—classic black
and white we pinned above our dorm room desks—
we knew a storm brewed, spinning weathervanes
and hustling flocks from sky to sky. We dozed,
most nights, nose deep in paperback
prognoses. *Wretched* and *Black Skin, White Masks*,
our books of revelation. Clarions
to would-be warriors, if only we
might rise up from our armchairs, lecture halls,
or blunt smoke cyphers. Talking all that gun
and glory, not a Nat among us. Free
to wax heroic. Deep. As bullet holes
through Panther posters, Huey's shattered throne.

"Poems are bullshit unless they are teeth..."
—*Amiri Baraka*

It ain't enough to rabble-rouse. To run
off at the mouth. To speechify and sing.
Just ain't enough to preach it, Poet, kin
to kin, pulpit to choir, as if song
were anything like Panther work. It ain't.
This morning when the poets took the park
to poet at each other, rage and rant,
the goon squad watched and smiled, watched us shake
our fists and fret. No doubt amused. As when
a mastiff meets a yapping lapdog, or
the way a king might watch a circus clown
produce a pistol from a passing car.
Our wrath the flag that reads *kaboom!* Our art,
a Malcolm poster rolled up, raised to swat.

"every once in a while
i see the winged spirits of niggas past raise out the rubble"
—Paul Beatty

Could be he meant to set the world right.
One bullet at a time. One well-placed slug,
one dancing shell case at a time. One hot
projectile pushing through, one body bag
zipped shut and shipped to cold store at a time.
Could be he meant to make us proud, to fill
Nat Turner's shoes. Could be he meant to aim
at each acquittal, scot-free cop, each trigger pull
or chokehold left unchecked, and blast daylight
straight through. Could be he meant, for once, to do.
We chat. We chant. We theorize and write.
We clasp our hands, spark frankincense, and pray.
Our gods, though, have no ears. And yet, his gun
sang loud. Enough to make them all lean in.

"Paradise is a world where everything is sanctuary & nothing is a gun."
—Danez Smith

A pipe bomb hurled through a wig shop's glass—
nine melting mannequins, nine crowns of flame.
Hair singe miasma, black smoke braided. Scream
of squad cars blocks away. Burnt out Caprice
and overturned Toyota. Strip mall stripped.
And gutted. Gift shop, pet shop, liquor store,
old stationery wholesale. Home decor,
cheap dinnerware. An old man sprinting, draped
in handbags, loaded down with wedding gowns.
Three Bloods and two Crips tying, end-to-end,
one red, one blue, bandana. Freebase fiend
with grocery bags, new kicks, and name-brand jeans.
Spilled jug of milk against the curb, black cat
bent low to lap it. This, your world, burnt bright.

"I love the world, but my heart's been cheated."
                    —Cornelius Eady

He thought a prayer and a pistol grip
enough to get it done. Enough to get
him free. Get free or, dying, try. To stop
the bleeding. *Blood on leaves, blood at the root.*
I didn't root, exactly, when I heard
word spread. Word that he crept up, panther-like,
and let loose lead. A lot. Before he fled
the spot, then somewhere underground, let kick
his cannon one last time. "One Time," our name
for cops back at the crib. It had to do,
I think, with chance. Or lack of. Chickens come
to roost? Perhaps. I didn't root. Per se.
But almost cracked a smile that day. The news
like wind chimes on the breeze. Or shattered glass.

"We beg your pardon, America. We beg your pardon, once again."
—Gil Scott-Heron

To preach forgiveness in a burning church.
To nevermind the noose. To nurse one cheek
then turn the next. To run and fetch the switch.
To switch up, weary of it all. Then cock
the hammer back and let it fall... But they
were men, you say, with children. And so close
to Christmas. But their wives, you say. Today
so close to Christmas... Memory as noose,
and history as burning church, who'd come
across the two cops parked and not think, *Go
time? One time for Tamir time?* Not think *Fire
this time?* To say as much is savage. Blame
the times, and what they've made of us. We know
now, which, and where—the pistol or the prayer.

"…like sparklers tracing an old alphabet in the night sky"
                                    —Amaud Jamaul Johnson

It's natural, no, to put your faith in fire?
The way it makes new all it touches. How
a city, let's say, might become, by way
of time and riot, pure. In '92,
we thought to gather ashes where before
loomed all that meant to kill us. Rubble now
and lovely. Worked into, as if from clay,
some sort of monument. To what? No clue.
Scorched earth, and then…? Suppose a man sets out,
with gun and half a plan, to be of use.
To hunt police. Insane, we'd say. Not long
for life. In this, we'd miss the point. A lit
match put to gas-soaked rag, the bottle flung,
may die, but dying, leaves a burning house.

"Afro angels, black saints, balanced upon the switchblades of that air and sang."
—*Robert Hayden*

But that was when you still believed in fire,
the gospel of the purge, the burning house.
You used to think a rifle and a prayer,
a pipe bomb hurled through a shopkeep's glass,
enough, at last, to set the world right.
Enough, at least, to galvanize some kin.
Think Malcolm at the window, set to shoot,
or Huey on his high-back wicker throne.
Think Normandy and Florence, brick in hand,
a black man dancing for the camera crews.
You change the channel, there he is again,
and begging: Find some bottles, fill with gas.
Begs breathe in deep the Molotov's perfume.
Says strike your one good match, then watch it bloom.

III

Another Monday and you're out
with some poets, one of whom—
maybe you—has just given a reading,
and it's summer and it's Brooklyn,
or it's the Village and it's winter,
and you've landed at some dusky,
dusty dive bar, crowded around
an eight-top to order wings, shots,
and whatnot, when, halfway down
the table, you hear one poet
congratulate a second on some prize
or another while a third sulks,
sips his gimlet and pretends not
to listen, and a fourth mumbles
something about not being notified
his application was even received
and how you have to be gay or
black or both to win anything
these days and a fifth poet pushes
a plate of nachos toward you
and asks what you think about
the state of Contemporary American
Poetry and, before you can answer,
a sixth pries in, mishearing of course

the last few syllables and waxes
cerebral, something about Don Share,
or *Ploughshares*, or maybe even
time shares and on the television
mounted, hanging overhead,
an anchorwoman's mouthing
the muted news of another boy
shot dead and black in some city
now burning and the police chief
promises a thorough investigation
and a Yemeni woman is burning,
splashed with acid for loving who
she chooses, and everywhere,
you think, is burning, burning and
Yes, you hear a graduate student quip
between slurps about a newly dead
master, *I tried to like his work—*
may he rest in peace—but try as I
might, I found him too accessible.
Another Monday and it's summer
in Brooklyn, or it's the Village
and winter. You're with the poets.
One of whom—the political poet,
the outsider poet—has brought along

a selfie stick. You put your shot glass
to your mouth. What's inside is burning,
burning. Everybody, now, squeeze in
tight. Everybody, now, say cheese.

ON EPIPHANY

as when, having rented a room
in the strangest part of a strange city,
    a space I'd share with an old black
piano, heirloom of the absentee tenants,
    I sit at and lift from the keys a thick
film of dust I rub between forefinger
    and thumb, and, trying to conjure
one song, am reminded of another,
    fading to the record's black static,
the precise moment I told a woman
    I was leaving, for good, then after
so much flimflam, stalked the streets
    of that other city, and was spun around
three blocks south, by said woman,
    who left two toddlers sleeping, alone,
to come chase me down, and how
    I left her again, alone, in the slow rain
falling, like some clichéd rom-com,
    and for no reason other than I was
a motherfucker, and playing my part
    in a parable old as the first woman, first
man, first snake and betrayal, first urge
    turned to ballad, to say something
what could ease that rain, or this, a tune

I can't remember, but whose notes
I know, just as I know I've no idea,
really, how to touch a piano.

AFTER THE DANCE

—after Ernie Barnes, *Sugar Shack*, circa 1971

Here, says a card shark spreading a map, are the rest
of your days laid out. Of course, the lines are faded.
The valleys, now, overgrown with havoc and industry,
the seven unnamable roads rubbed to faint music
in the back of an old man's mind. Was there a town
there? A woman he once loved? The lights go dim
and the band strikes up. But loneliness, you think,
is its own small city. A gravedigger sidles up, offers
to pay for your dinner. I'm drinking it, you say,
then bank a bedroom stare, off the dusty mirror floating
over the barhop's shoulder, at the one-armed drummer
grinning from the bandstand. He's in the pocket.
He's getting down. His hand is a blur of bad intentions
when he blows you six kisses. You uncross
and cross your legs. I run a sanctuary for out-of-work
morticians, the gravedigger says. Of course, you ignore
the gravedigger. Just like you ignore the four drunk
church ladies glaring from the cheap seats, and hike
your skirt just a little bit more. An oil lamp sputters
on every table in the joint. Reflected near every flame,
a crooked gold tooth. You check the bandstand again,
try to catch the drummer's eye. But he's eyeing thighs
on the other side of the room. Shorter skirt, skinnier
waist on a younger, faster, you. If loneliness, Lady,

is an old world city, tonight you're set to be mayor.
All the walls sweat when the lights come up. Last call,
and the gravedigger's disappeared with your pocketbook.

VARIATION ON A THEME BY GIL SCOTT-HERON

Near midnight mid-December,
and the soldier, my junkie uncle,
    sleepwalks home. Up avenues
strewn with everyday debris,
    past rats he imagines man-made
and robot. In his heavy half sleep,
    he palms, barely, a bone knife stolen
from the dead butcher's meat shop.
    Gris-gris against the bandits
in his head, the hounds at his heels.
    There's a rumble, now, rising
from behind the old armory.
    A black chopper lifting,
lighting up the block. It hovers
    like a hummingbird bred for death.
When he points it out to passersby,
    they laugh or look away. He points
again, of course it's gone. The one
    good cloud he can still make out
is where his god resides. That's
    the good news. The bad news
is that his god has got three trained
    snipers beaming from a rooftop.
In each one's crosshairs, uncle soldier

ducks and staggers. Early winter,
his breath is bonedust. Decorated
   war dog whose only friends are ghosts.
But even they, tonight, are elsewhere.

ON LYRIC NARRATIVE

The applejack caps of aging players dusted
with February's first, the fur and faux-leather collars
yanked up around their ears—I see one among them,
my father, philosophizing in the bleak light
of a street lamp, shoulders hunched, shifting his weight
from one foot to the other, begging
a smoke from the gold-toothed gunrunner.
And there, in the middle of the men, a blazing oilcan
around which they'll croon to the cruel stars,
disinterested moon. And soon, the gunrunner reaches
for a cigarette, a lighter. My father leans into
the man's cupped hands and his whole face glows.
A six-inch switchblade catches in the shadow
just behind and to the left of my father and here,
here is where I force myself awake. Were my father alive,
I'd call the house and warn him: Watch your back.
Trust no one. And how well do you know
the gunrunner? But it's twenty-seven winters
since we laid him down. Besides, he never was one
to put much stock in visions. Voodoo, he'd say.
You want to help me, help me hit the numbers, he'd say.
My philosophy professors would have called him
an empiricist. He believed in what he laid his hands on.
My mother. A cigarette. A crumpled dollar bill.

An applejack cap pulled low against the wind.
My wife almost wakes. I pull her close, then drift.
If everyone in a dream, as I read once, represents
the dreamer, what was my father trying to tell me?
When am I the gunrunner? When am I the wind?
When the snow, the moon, or the switchblade's glint?

DISTANT LOVER (OR, WHEN YOU'RE TEACH-
ING IN AMHERST AND, WHILE ON A LATE NIGHT
WALK, YOUR WIFE CALLS FROM BROOKLYN TO
SAY GOODNIGHT)

The dead of February, and everything sexual.

So sexual the icicles skirting the barn.

Sexual the animals huddled inside, shivering.

Sexual the cloud disappearing, appearing

again, from your half-open mouth. The moon

swollen bright. Sexual the trees, stark

naked, all their branches spread and undulating

in the wind. Sexual the tundra. Sexual

the blackest snow by the road, made blacker

by the city worker's plow. Sexual, the snowman

leaning in a midnight yard. So sexual

dead February, the small town windows lit

from inside, fogging, watching you burn.

ON PROSODY

Dawn again. And this is what we wake to.
Neighbors' ruckus through our bedroom wall—
a tussle, something breaking. And, of course,
the voices. This, this din, is what we wake to
almost every Sunday, no? Such fear,
such chronic angers. Same as those that haunted
Robert Hayden. Here, this morning, though,
I'm thinking more of Robert Frost. His letters,
the *sound of sense*. What Frost says we can glean
from pitch and speech's rhythms, hearing through
a wall—not making out a single word—
what neighbors say and mean.
                                    This morning, like
the rest, they mean to hurt. A wife, her husband.
Fisticuffs and hollers. We think they fight
about the kids, or unpaid bills, or fight
because on mornings off they hear us too—
not fighting—and remember. Rapture then,
and rupture now. These offices of love.
"Not meters," Frost said, "but a meter-making
argument." Or was that Emerson?
In any case, we press our ears, with glass,
against the wall, and learn the man's not half
the man his brother is. The wife's a whore

the husband swears he'll kill. Like clockwork. Same
as any Sunday. Still, we call the cops,
they come and go. Our neighbors break then start
again by dusk. And this is how we've learned
to measure time. Not hours, but each rage
and all the intervals between.

                        By now
I've told you all about my father's hands.
His leather. All those nights our neighbors must
have thought I'd die. But there was quiet, too—
a Sunday just like this, my father sprawled
across the couch; my mother, me, the black
and white TV, kept mute all afternoon.
To anyone who might be listening,
we could have been the Cleavers. Waltons. Rapt
in bible study, homework, corny arts
and crafts. A slant of sunlight stabbing through
the curtains, catching Mom's good china, Fido's
easy breathing. But you know me, now,
enough to know this ain't that story. Think,
instead, a love song. *If I can't have you . . .*
and such. Our quiet broken into when
the neighbors hit the high notes.

                          Rumor was

Latoya caught her husband creeping—with
the deacon's boy—and made him choose. He broke
things off, or didn't, or denied the whole
affair, or didn't, or he might have tried
to string them both along, or wasn't clear
enough to one, or either, till one day
the lover shows up on his doorstep, high,
they say, on Angel Dust. On Angel Dust
and loneliness. A Sunday just like this.
I'm six. And so, I'm keen to none of it.
The details, I mean. This much I remember:
a knock that shook my father from his sleep…
a grown man's cry . . . a scuffle . . . muffled cuss
and crash . . . and then . . . the baby. Braying. Like
a small goat led to slaughter.

                              I pressed my ear,
and then my chest and palms against the wall,
and took in all his suffering, all his fear,
how one who leads said goat will feel its heart
beat through its chest, and carry that for days
in hands he can't scrub clean. Or like the boy
I read of once—composer's son born deaf—
who, on the day his father died, replayed
his father's favorite album, dusk to dawn,

until the grooves wore smooth, and all the while
he bit down on the speakerbox's edge,
so music traveled from his teeth, along his jaw,
into a skull so taken with the song
the boy, himself, became that song. So, too,
did I, when pressed against the wall, become
the room next door, and everything it held—
each crashing dish, each welt and scratch, the odd
caesura
        when the infant hit the wall.

Something, Frost says, doesn't love a wall.
But something too, goddammit, wishes walls
within the walls and more walls after that.
My mother called the cops. Of course, they came
and went. But not before my father kicked
the neighbors' door to splinters, beat the husband,
lover—each, perhaps—until the blue lights,
red lights, painted every wall. Of course,
the cops took all the men away. So, too,
the child and mother left. For good. And left
behind a silence I still carry, hands
I can't scrub clean, so taken with the song
I am, in fact, the song.

We wrap these sheets
around us. Soundless. Lie here as if sheltered.
As if so much wood and gypsum, nails and
peeling paint, might keep next door, next door.
As if I haven't brought here, to this room,
into this bed, these hands and all they've borne.
And maybe this is, insofar as there's
a point, the point. Forgive my rambling and
the sun its breaking in. It's dawn again
and you should rest. Besides, they're done
next door. For now, at least. No shrieks, no shouts.
No other brutal music.
                            Dawn again
and, lying, we can hear the city wake—
One homeboy hails another. Trash trucks groan
and sigh. Two grackles greet, then call across
the rooftops to an ugly cousin. All
indoors, though, this or that side of the wall,
is hushed half light, this next day coming on
like all the ones before. This hushed half light
that finds our neighbors lying, maybe, same
as us. Her breasts against his back. His chest
against her back. Two knees, now, nestled tight
into the crooks of other knees. His droning

on, as he caresses, just like this,
her temple. Same as any Sunday. When
I slip my arm, half numb, from underneath,
you stir and almost wake. I take myself
and all my troubles to the window. Light
this blunt then watch the block. Another day.
Another day with you, and not a clue
what we might do.

VARIATION ON A THEME BY THE NOTORIOUS B.I.G.

It was all a dream. I used to read AGNI magazine—
Martín Espada, Komunyakaa, Philip Levine.
Gripped by dreams of growing to rock a rhyme,
picked up steam when I seen *Where a Nickel Costs a Dime*.
Spent my time weekdays and weekends,
thinking of ways of freakin' the Nuyorican.
Thursdays were my worst days,
'cause I had my workshop. But the work paid.

Now I seek the limelight, hope my rhymes might
take me from born sinner to fancy award winner.
From sardines for dinner straight to champagne toasts,
gala seats, meet-and-greets, all down the east coast.
Changed my ways now it's all in reach—
till I pen my nigger pain and they snatch my seat.

NOTES

"Variation on a Theme by Elizabeth Bishop" is inspired by, and borrows lines from, Bishop's poem "One Art."

The first and last lines of "Poem Ending and Beginning on Lines by Larry Levis" are from Levis' poems, "The Spirit Says You Are Nothing" and "Slow Child with a Book of Birds," respectively. It also contains a prayer for the Yoruba Orisha, Ogun. San Quentin, Soledad, and Folsom are California prisons.

"Dear Yusef," is dedicated to poet Yusef Komunyakaa.

"Mercy, Mercy Me" was written soon after the twenty-fifth anniversary of the Los Angeles Uprisings of 1992, commonly known as "The Rodney King Riots."

The title "A Refusal to Mourn the Deaths, by Gunfire, of Three Men in Brooklyn" is a nod to Dylan Thomas' famous poem, "A Refusal to Mourn the Death, by Fire, of a Child in London." The poem itself was written in part as a reflection on police-community relations since the 1992 uprisings, and partly as a response to the killing of two NYPD officers and subsequent suicide of twenty-eight year old Ishmael Brinsley. On December 20, 2014, Brinsley shot and killed Brooklyn officers Rafael Ramos and Wenjian Liu, before fleeing the scene and ultimately shooting himself dead on a subway platform. Brinsley had also shot and wounded his ex-girlfriend before boarding a bus that morning from Baltimore to New York City. His attack on the officers was reportedly motivated by the rash of police killings of unarmed black people nationwide. Coincidentally, while Brinsley was carrying out his attack, poets were gathered in New York's Washington Square Park to read poems in protest of said killings.

"Variation on a Theme by Gil Scott-Heron" is inspired by, and based loosely on, lines from Scott-Heron's poem/song "Home Is Where the Hatred Is."

"Variation on a Theme by the Notorious B.I.G." contains elements of the song "Juicy" written by Christopher Wallace, a.k.a., The Notorious B.I.G. *Where a Nickel Costs a Dime* is the title of Willie Perdomo's first poetry collection.

"Mercy, Mercy Me," "After the Dance," and "Distant Lover" borrow their titles from Marvin Gaye songs.

ACKNOWLEDGMENTS

Maferefun Olofi, Maferefun Olodumare, Maferefun Elegba, Maferefun Obatala, Maferefun Oshun, Maferefun Shango, Maferefun Oya, Maferefun Yemaya, Maferefun Ogun, Maferefun Ochosi, Maferefun Aganju, Maferefun Ibeji, Maferefun Gbogbo Orisha, Maferefun Gbogbo Egun. Modupwe Padrino Eshu Adewa, Modupwe Ojubona Oshun Atiliwa, Modupwe Ile Ashe—elders, siblings, and godchildren. Alafia.

Many thanks to the editors of the following publications in which some of these poems first appeared, sometimes in slightly different versions:

Academy of American Poets Poem-a-Day, American Poetry Review, The Common, The Iowa Review, jubilat, Los Angeles Review, Ploughshares, Poetry, Prairie Schooner, Provincetown Arts, River Styx, and *Washington Square Review.*

"Upon Reading That Eric Dolphy Transcribed Even the Calls of Certain Species of Birds" also appears in *Best American Poetry 2017.*

"On Confessionalism" also appears in *Best American Poetry 2019.*

"Upon Reading That Eric Dolphy Transcribed Even the Calls of Certain Species of Birds" also appears in *The Mind Has Cliffs of Fall: Poetry at the Extremes of Feeling,* W.W. Norton, 2019.

"Variation on a Theme by Elizabeth Bishop" also appears in *Furious Flower: Seeding the Future of African-American Poetry,* Northwestern University Press, 2019.

"Upon Reading That Eric Dolphy Transcribed Even the Calls of Certain Species of Birds" "On Confessionalism," and "Dolores, Maybe" also appear in *What Saves Us: Poems of Empathy and Outrage in the Age of Trump,* Northwestern University Press, 2019.

Gratitude to everyone who helped these poems along: Reginald Dwayne Betts, Traci Brimhall, Jericho Brown, Joel Dias-Porter, Martín Espada, Ross Gay, Terrance Hayes, Tyehimba Jess, Brandon D. Johnson, A. Van Jordan, Janine Joseph, David Tomas Martinez, Adrian Matejka, Sami Miranda, Willie Perdomo, Patrick Rosal, Nicole Sealey, and Jeanann Verlee.

Gratitude to the following organizations and institutions for time, space, resources, and support: Atlantic Center for the Arts, Bread Loaf Writers' Conference, Cave Canem Foundation, Fine Arts Work Center in Provincetown, The Frost Place, MacDowell Colony, the National Endowment for the Arts, the Poetry Foundation, Poets House, Hampshire College School for Interdisciplinary Arts, New York University Creative Writing Program, and Wesleyan University.

Gratitude to the phenomenal Derrick Adams for blessing the cover. Gratitude to Marcus Jackson for making me look pretty.

Gratitude to the fam at Four Way Books for making this happen: Martha Rhodes, Sally Ball, Ryan Murphy, and Clarissa Long.

Shoutout to The Stairwell Crew, a.k.a. The Brotherhood, a.k.a. The Stagolee Underground.

Utmost, infinite, and insufficient gratitude to Nicole Sealey. My heart, my life.